Long-Distance Communication

Mary Hertz Scarbrough

BLACKBIRCH®
PRESS

THOMSON

GALE

San Diego • Detroit • New York • San Francisco • Cleveland • New Haven, Conn. • Waterville, Maine • London • Munich

For more information, contact
The Gale Group, Inc.
27500 Drake Rd.
Farmington Hills, MI 48331-3535
Or you can visit our Internet site at http://www.gale.com

Picture Credits
Cover: © Bettmann/CORBIS (top), © Art Today, Inc. (bottom)
© Art Today, Inc., 11 (inset), 13, 15 (both), 16, 23, 26 (top), 27, 29, 30, 31
© Bettmann/CORBIS, 7, 14, 18, 24
© Jim Bourg/Reuters, 26 (bottom)
Dover Publications, 12 (top)
© Mary Evans/Edwin Wallace, 9 (inset)
Library of Congress, 5, 20
NASA, 19, 22 (both)
© North Wind Picture Archives, 4

© Photo Disc, Inc., 12 (bottom)
© Reunion des Musees Nationaux/ Art Resource, NY, 6, 9 (bottom)
Reuters, 25
© Schenectady Museum; Hall of Electrical History Foundation/CORBIS, 21
© The Schøyen Collection, 8
© Leonard de Selva/CORBIS, 10
Jayanta Shaw/Reuters, 28
© Smithsonian Institution, 17
© Stocktrek/CORBIS, 11 (bottom)

LIBRARY OF CONGRESS CATALOGING-IN-PUBLICATION DATA

Scarbrough, Mary Hertz
    Long-distance communication / by Mary Hertz Scarbrough.
        p. cm. — (Yesterday and today)
    Includes bibliographical references.
    ISBN 1-56711-832-1 (hardback : alk. paper)
    1. Telecommunication—History—Juvenile literature. I. Title. II. Series.

    TK5102.4.S33 2004
    621.382—dc22   2004008269

Printed in the United States
10 9 8 7 6 5 4 3 2 1

Table of Contents

Long-Distance Signals

Early humans could not read or write, nor did they have the technology we have today. Long-distance communication was difficult. The receiver of a message had to be close enough to the sender to see or hear the message.

Spoken messages could be sent only as far as they could be heard. People sometimes shouted from one hilltop to another. They even imitated animal sounds to send messages.

Before people could read or write, Native Americans often used signal fires and smoke signals to send messages over long distances.

Some people used talking drums to send coded messages. The sound of the drumbeats imitated the rhythm and tone of spoken words. These messages could be heard up to five miles away. Native American and African tribes have both used drums to communicate.

People can usually see much farther than they can hear, so visible messages were important in prehistoric times. People waved their arms, flags, blankets, or lances to send messages others could see. They also flashed reflected sunlight to send signals. Native Americans sometimes made special movements while on horseback as a way to signal others.

People sometimes signaled to others with torches. The ancient Jewish book, the Talmud, tells about people who lit a chain of fires on hilltop after hilltop to carry a message far away.

The Great Plains Indians used smoke signals to send messages during the day. They used a blanket to cover and uncover a smoky fire. The number of puffs of smoke could mean different things. For example, three puffs of smoke could mean that an enemy was nearby. More puffs could mean more danger. The smoke could be seen as far as sixty miles away.

Paul Revere used a light signal to warn the American patriots that British soldiers were coming.

A Historic Signal

One of the most famous moments in American history involved a light signal. Henry Wadsworth Longfellow's poem "Paul Revere's Ride," describes how American patriots learned of the plans of British soldiers on April 18, 1775:

> He said to his friend, "If the British march
> By land or sea from the town to-night,
> Hang a lantern aloft in the belfry arch
> Of the North church tower as a signal light,—
> One if by land, and two if by sea.

Prehistory —

500 B.C. —

100 B.C. —

A.D. 100 —

200 —

500 —

1000 —

1200 —

1300 —

1400 —

1500 —

1600 —

1700 —

1800 —

1900 —

2000 —

2100 —

Carrying Messages from One Place to Another

In this silk painting a messenger delivers a letter using one of the earliest postal systems, which developed in China around 900 B.C.

Although torches, talking drums, smoke signals, and other methods were sometimes used to send messages, the most common way to deliver a message was in person. Even before writing was invented, messengers traveled far and wide to deliver spoken messages. One drawback was that spoken messages could be forgotten or mixed up before the messenger arrived at the destination.

For many centuries, messages moved only as quickly as the messengers who carried them. Messengers walked, rode horses, or traveled by boat. China had a postal system by 900 B.C. Persia's postal system in the fifth century B.C. was particularly well organized. Royal messengers traveled between stations about fourteen miles apart. About two thousand years ago, the Roman emperor Augustus established a postal system. Couriers traveled to northern Europe, Asia, and Spain. They rode horseback or on horse-drawn carts called chariots.

Augustus's postal system lasted until the fifth century A.D. Afterward, some monasteries and universities set up messenger services for their own use. Europe had no other postal service until 1305, when the Taxis family of Italy started a private service. Emperors, military officers, and merchants throughout Europe used the service. About 150 years later, King Louis XI established a postal service in France.

Ships carried mail to Europe and then back again from the American colonies. The letters were delivered to taverns and coffeehouses. After a ship came into port, people stopped by the tavern to collect their mail.

During World War I, American soldiers used carrier pigeons to deliver messages that saved many lives.

Prehistory ——

500 B.C. ——

100 B.C. ——

A.D. 100 ——

200 ——

500 ——

1000 ——

1200 ——

1300 ——

1400 ——

1500 ——

1600 ——

1700 ——

1800 ——

1900 ——

2000 ——

2100 ——

Homing or carrier pigeons have carried messages for thousands of years. During the first Olympics in 776 B.C., the birds flew from Athens to other cities with written news of the winners. Long before the Olympics, the birds delivered messages for the Egyptian military. The U.S. military even used the birds during the twentieth century. During World War I, one bird named Cher Ami helped save nearly two hundred trapped soldiers. It managed to deliver an important message even though it had been seriously wounded by enemy fire.

FAST FACT

President George Washington sent the first airmail letter in America when he sent a letter on the first hot air balloon trip in the Western Hemisphere in 1793. Regular airmail service began in 1918 between New York and Washington, D.C.

Printing

The invention of writing meant that messages could be sent without worry that the messenger would forget the message. The earliest writing systems required memorization of hundreds of pictographs (picture symbols). Each pictograph could have many meanings.

The earliest known alphabet comes from Egypt and dates from around 1900–1800 B.C. Its thirty symbols represent sounds from the spoken language. Even with the alphabet, few people could read and write. Scribes wrote messages for people who could not write, and made copies of documents.

Because copying by hand took so much time, people looked for faster ways to make copies. A primitive printing process was developed. First, the printers chiseled words or characters into smooth stones. They then pressed dampened paper over the chiseled stone. When the paper dried, it retained the character indentations from the stone. Next, the paper was inked, but the indentations stayed white. Finally, clean paper was pressed against the inked paper. The result was white characters set against a dark background. All these steps took a long time, however.

People could print more quickly when they began to make stamps out of wood blocks. The raised characters or letters were inked and then pressed on sheets to make copies.

During the eleventh century in China, Pi Sheng invented a moveable type. It was called moveable because each baked clay character was separate and could be reused. The invention was not very useful in China, however. The Chinese language had thousands of characters, and a printer needed separate type for each one.

Some of the earliest writing consisted of symbols chiseled into stone. The carving on this stone dates from around 1750 B.C.

Scribes (left) wrote messages for people who could not write. Messengers then carried the letters if they had to be delivered over long distances.

Prehistory —

500 B.C. —

100 B.C. —

A.D. 100 —

200 —

500 —

1000 —

1200 —

1300 —

1400 —

1500 —

1600 —

1700 —

1800 —

1900 —

2000 —

2100 —

Around 1450 in Germany, Johannes Gutenberg invented a successful moveable type and a wooden printing press. Gutenberg made individual letters out of metal. He spelled words with these letters and set them in rows on a wooden frame. The letters, or type, were inked. Then a sheet of damp paper was pressed on the type. The words were now printed on the paper. The process was repeated on the other side of the paper.

The printing press saved money and time. A printer could do in one or two days what it would take a scribe a year to do. Gutenberg's invention made written communication much more widely available.

Copying Characters

Gutenberg devised a way to make molds for the printing press's letters and characters. The molds allowed him to make many copies of the letters and characters. Unlike the Chinese version, Gutenberg's printing press needed only about fifty characters to set type.

Claude Chappe invented the semaphore, which sent visual messages to stations several miles away.

A Long-Lived Invention

Chappe called his invention the *telegraphe*, which means "far writer." It became better known as the semaphore. *Semaphore* comes from the Greek words for "carry" and "signals." The railroads and the U.S. Navy still use modified versions of Chappe's invention. In the navy, messengers use half-red, half-yellow flags to signal between ships.

The Semaphore

Even though messengers and postal systems were useful, people still wanted to be able to send messages farther and more quickly. The invention of the semaphore in 1791 meant messages could travel much faster than ever before.

Even as a child growing up in France, Claude Chappe was interested in ways to improve long-distance communication. As an adult, he used ancient visual signaling ideas and then improved upon them with his invention of the semaphore.

The semaphore was a T-shaped device that was placed on top of a tower or other high spot. A short wing was attached to each end of the crossbar of the T. Both the crossbar of the T and the short wings could be placed in different positions. These different positions represented different letters or words, according to the code Chappe had invented.

Several miles away a man would wait at another station. This man would read the message with the help of a telescope. He would then repeat the message to the next station up the line. The message could be forwarded to as many stations as necessary to deliver it.

Chappe and one of his brothers demonstrated an early version of the invention for the French government in 1791. They sent a message ten miles away in about four minutes. The French government was impressed. It built a fifteen-station line from Paris to Lille. It only took about two minutes for a semaphore message to travel the 130-mile distance. After Napoléon Bonaparte came to power in France in 1799, he built more and more stations.

Other countries soon copied Chappe's design, or came up with their own. By the mid-1830s, Europe had nearly one thousand semaphore towers spread out over three thousand miles.

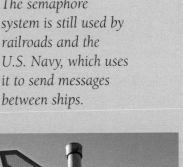

The semaphore system is still used by railroads and the U.S. Navy, which uses it to send messages between ships.

Prehistory

500 B.C.

100 B.C.

A.D. 100

200

500

1000

1200

1300

1400

1500

1600

1700

1800

1900

2000

2100

11

The Telegraph

The semaphore was soon replaced by something that could deliver messages faster and farther. For many years, some inventors had believed that coded messages could be sent through electrical wires. By the mid-1830s everything necessary for such a machine had been invented. All that was missing was an inventor who could put the pieces together.

Samuel Morse was a painter and writer who knew nothing about electricity. While aboard a ship in the early 1830s, he heard about electric signal experiments other inventors had tried. Fascinated, he decided to work on the idea himself. He created a signaling code made up of dots and dashes and called it Morse code. Morse also enlisted the help of two others: an inventor, Joseph Henry, and a mechanic, Alfred Vail. The three created a machine that could transmit electrical signals in Morse code in 1837. It was called the telegraph.

Meanwhile, two inventors in England developed their own telegraph machine at the same time as Morse. The English inventors were William Fothergill Cooke and Charles Wheatstone.

The American and English telegraphs had different designs but worked on the same principles. The telegraph had two parts, a transmitter and a receiver. These were connected by wire. On the transmitter, a telegraph key worked as a switch to turn the electric current on and off. A person tapped the key to make long and short pulses. These electric pulses traveled through the wire to the receiver. At the receiver, the message was decoded in different ways. In Morse's telegraph, a special pen wrote the pulses, called dots and dashes, on a strip of paper. The receiving operator could also hear the dots and dashes. In the English

Samuel Morse (above) invented a code to send signals through electrical wires. He worked with Joseph Henry and Alfred Vail to create the telegraph machine.

version, magnetized needles pointed to letters that corresponded to the dots and dashes.

In both countries, the invention caught on slowly. People thought it was interesting but not very useful. Opinions changed quickly in England in 1845, when a murderer escaped by train to London. Police arrested the man when he arrived. They knew what he looked like because his description had been telegraphed ahead.

In the United States, the first transcontinental telegraph line was finished in October 1861. Telegraph messages could then be sent from coast to coast. The Pony Express, which carried mail from Missouri to the American West on horseback, could not compete with the telegraph. It soon went out of business.

Soon after the invention of the telegraph, a transcontinental telegraph line allowed messages to be sent quickly from one coast to the other.

FAST FACT

It took several tries, but telegraph lines finally connected North America and Europe in 1866. Ships laid cables underneath the Atlantic Ocean.

Prehistory

500 B.C.

100 B.C.

A.D. 100

200

500

1000

1200

1300

1400

1500

1600

1700

1800

1900

2000

2100

The Telephone

Alexander Graham Bell originally wanted to make a telegraph that could send more than one message at a time. Instead, in 1876, he invented the telephone.

Bell's telegraph experiments got sidetracked when he became intrigued by a different idea. He wanted to send a human voice over a wire. Bell was neither a scientist nor an engineer, however. He had originally been a teacher of the deaf. He needed someone to help make his ideas work. Bell found a young mechanic named Thomas Watson to help him. Watson knew a great deal about electricity. He had the skills to make Bell's idea come to life.

By the middle of 1875, Bell and Watson could send sound over a wire, but they could not send speech that could be understood. They finally succeeded on March 9, 1876. Watson was in another room when Bell shouted into the telephone, "Mr. Watson, come here. I want you." For the first time, Watson could understand the voice at the other end.

A Lucky Break

Bell patented his invention but was short of money afterward. He tried to sell the telephone to Western Union for $100,000. The telegraph company turned him down, but this turned out to be good for Bell. The telephone soon became popular. Today, it is the world's most widely used means of long-distance communication.

After the invention of the telegraph, Alexander Graham Bell figured out a way to send the sound of the human voice over electrical wires.

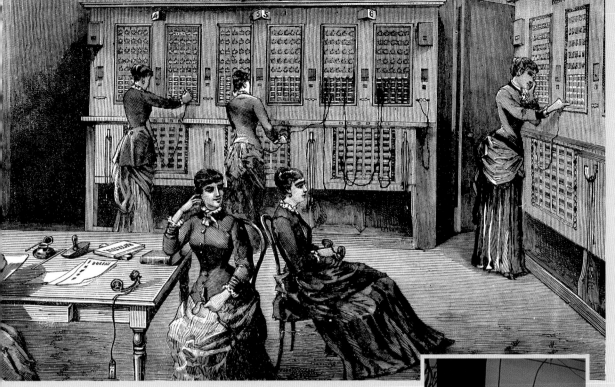

A person's speech creates sound waves. Sound waves are vibrations in the air. Different sounds make the air vibrate at different speeds. A microphone in a telephone's mouthpiece changes sound waves from a speaker's voice into electrical signals. It does this with a thin metal piece called a diaphragm. The sound waves make the diaphragm vibrate. Electric current in the mouthpiece changes the sound waves into electrical signals. These signals are transmitted swiftly over the telephone line to the receiving telephone.

Within the earpiece of a telephone is a receiver that turns the electrical signal back into understandable speech. The electric current hits a magnet in the receiver and creates a magnetic field. The magnet is attached to another diaphragm. The magnetic field attracts the diaphragm and makes it move in and out. This movement pulls and pushes the air in front of it. This movement of air is sound waves that can now be heard. The receiver re-creates the sound waves spoken at the other end of the line.

Bell and Thomas Watson invented the telephone in 1876 and soon phone wires crisscrossed the country. It quickly became the best way to communicate over long distances.

Prehistory ⎯

500 B.C. ⎯

100 B.C. ⎯

A.D. 100 ⎯

200 ⎯

500 ⎯

1000 ⎯

1200 ⎯

1300 ⎯

1400 ⎯

1500 ⎯

1600 ⎯

1700 ⎯

1800 ⎯

1900 ⎯

2000 ⎯

2100 ⎯

15

The Wireless Telegraph

The telephone improved long-distance communication, but it relied on wires for a connection. Some inventors began to explore the possibility of wireless communication.

In 1894, a twenty-year-old Italian named Guglielmo Marconi began to study electricity and electromagnetic waves (electric waves that travel through space). He learned that an electric current in one wire could create a current in another wire, even when the wires did not touch. He thought the theories he studied could be used to improve long-distance communication.

Electrical signals can be sent through the air and received with metal aerials, or antennae. When electrical signals are transmitted from aerials, they create electromagnetic waves in the air. The waves are reflected back to earth by earth's atmosphere and are picked up by receiving antennae.

Marconi was able to send wireless signals more than one mile away within a year after he began to experiment. He transmitted radio waves in long and short pulses. These pulses came into the receiver as dots and dashes, as in Morse code.

The Italian government was not very interested in Marconi's experiments, so he moved to England. In 1898, Marconi found the perfect place to show off his

Guglielmo Marconi used radio waves to send wireless messages, which improved long-distance communication.

16

wireless telegraph. Queen Victoria of England was a fan of yacht races. During the Kingstown Yacht Regatta, Marconi placed a transmitter on a ship and sent reports to people onshore. He succeeded—he impressed the queen and the public.

In March 1899, Marconi transmitted signals across the English Channel. That same year the U.S. Navy tested the wireless and discovered that its signals could reach up to thirty-six miles from ship to ship. The wireless helped save many lives at sea, including hundreds who otherwise would have died when the ocean liner *Titanic* struck an iceberg in the North Atlantic Ocean in 1912.

Marconi wanted to prove that wireless signals could travel thousands of miles, even across oceans. No one completely understood how electromagnetic waves worked. Even respected scientists such as Thomas Edison did not believe Marconi could succeed. In late 1901, however, Marconi successfully transmitted transatlantic signals between Newfoundland, Canada, and Poldhu, England.

Telegrams

A telegram is a printed copy of a telegraph message. Telegrams were usually hand delivered to the recipient. They were most popular with businesses. Ordinary people usually used telegrams only for urgent messages. Telegrams were often used to tell relatives about a death in the family.

Although he did not completely understand how electromagnetic waves worked, in 1901 Marconi sent wireless signals between England and Canada.

Prehistory —

500 B.C. —

100 B.C. —

A.D. 100 —

200 —

500 —

1000 —

1200 —

1300 —

1400 —

1500 —

1600 —

1700 —

1800 —

1900 —

2000 —

2100 —

17

Radio

The invention of the wireless telegraph led directly to the invention of radio. Both the wireless telegraph and radio use the same technology.

Radio transmitters convert sounds into electromagnetic waves. These waves travel without wires through space to a receiving set, or radio. The radio converts the waves back into sounds. Listeners tune into a station that has been given a specific frequency. Frequency is the number of times the electromagnetic waves move up and down each second. Each broadcast station has its own frequency to prevent interference from other stations.

The first radio broadcast took place in 1906 in Brant Rock, Massachusetts. Reginald Fessenden used a specially designed transmitter to broadcast a Christmas greeting and carols to ships along the Atlantic coast. Wireless operators on the ships had been told to listen for the broadcast.

Although the sound was not clear, Reginald Fessenden sent the first radio broadcast in 1906.

Prehistory ——

500 B.C. ——

100 B.C. ——

A.D. 100 ——

200 ——

500 ——

1000 ——

1200 ——

1300 ——

1400 ——

1500 ——

1600 ——

1700 ——

1800 ——

1900 ——

2000 ——

2100 ——

Fessenden's broadcast was historic, but the sound was less than crystal clear. Lee De Forest is sometimes called the "Father of Radio," although many others, such as Marconi, played a part in its development. De Forest gave radio a boost when he patented an invention called the triode tube in 1907. A few years later he and others linked a chain of these tubes together. They discovered that the linked tubes strengthened weak radio signals.

Amateur radio operators began to broadcast music, speech, and coded messages around the country. After the United States entered World War I in 1917, however, the military took over radio for its own use for the duration of the war.

Amateur enthusiasts resumed their radio broadcasts after the war was over. The first radio station was KDKA in Pittsburgh, Pennsylvania. KDKA began in 1920 in the garage of a man named Frank Conrad.

Businesses began to take an interest in radio, and it grew swiftly. Some companies sold radio equipment. Others established radio stations. Companies began to pay to advertise on the radio. In 1922, there were only about three dozen stations in the United States. Before the year ended, there were hundreds.

Radio was very popular in the 1930s and through World War II. During the 1930s, radio programs helped people to forget about the Depression, the tough economic times then taking place in the United States. During the war, radio gave people up-to-date news from overseas and the president.

Astronauts on the moon sent messages to earth using electromagnetic waves, which made their communication truly long distance.

FAST FACT

The farthest long-distance communication between humans was between astronauts on the moon and Mission Control on earth. To communicate, they transmitted and received their messages on electromagnetic waves, just as a radio station sends messages to a person's radio.

19

Television

Television is related to radio, because both types of signals are carried on electromagnetic waves through the air. With television, the waves carry both sound and image signals. The television set converts the signals back into sound and images. Today, instead of being carried by radio waves, television signals are often transmitted by cable and satellite.

Television captures movement as a series of still images. The images are broken down into thousands of separate elements. This allows for their transmission as electrical signals. At the receiver, the signals are converted back into sounds and images. The human brain sees the rapid sequence of still images as one continuously moving image.

In the mid-1920s, Scottish inventor John Logic Baird demonstrated a simple television and convinced many doubters that television was possible. Baird first transmitted a still image, the head of a ventriloquist's dummy. Around the same time, Charles Jenkins in the United States transmitted the moving image of a windmill to a receiver five miles away. These early televisions had several shortcomings, including fuzzy and flickering images.

Many inventors experimented with ways to make television a reality. Two names often associated with the creation of television are Russian immigrant Vladimir Zworykin and a young man from Utah named Philo Farnsworth.

Farnsworth was born in 1905 and made his first working television when he was only twenty-one. He went on to obtain many patents connected with television development. Zworykin developed a receiver with a fluorescent

In the mid-1920s, Charles Jenkins transmitted moving images over electromagnetic waves, using the first television in the United States.

Prehistory ——

500 B.C. ——

100 B.C. ——

A.D. 100 ——

200 ——

500 ——

1000 ——

1200 ——

1300 ——

1400 ——

1500 ——

1600 ——

1700 ——

1800 ——

1900 ——

2000 ——

2100 ——

screen. Most modern televisions and computer screens still use Zworykin's technology.

Zworykin had an advantage over Farnsworth because he worked for the wealthy Radio Corporation of America (RCA). By 1939, RCA was ready to unveil television, and its exhibit at the World's Fair in New York gave many people their first glimpse of the new invention. Franklin Roosevelt was the first president to appear on television. He was televised delivering a speech during the fair.

As with radio, a world war interrupted television's development. Scientists and inventors needed to focus on wartime projects. After World War II ended, television usage soared. Color television began to replace black and white in the mid-1950s.

Many people saw television for the first time when it was exhibited at the New York World's Fair in 1939.

Satellites

Early satellites were sent into space using rockets.

A satellite is something that orbits, or circles, a planet. The moon is a natural satellite of earth because it orbits earth. Artificial satellites also orbit earth. These human-made inventions relay radio, television, telephone, and telegraph signals from one place on earth to another.

Satellites receive and transmit information with electromagnetic waves. A transmitting station on earth sends its signals to a satellite receiver. This is called an uplink. A satellite downlinks when it transmits signals to a receiver on earth.

Communications satellites receive information from one place on earth and transmit that information to another place on earth. Radio and television transmission and long-distance telephone calls are some of the uses of communications satellites. Other uses, such as video teleconferencing, allow people to talk face-to-face even when they are thousands of miles apart.

The Soviet Union was the first country to launch a satellite. It launched *Sputnik* on October 4, 1957. The United States launched *Explorer I* on January 31, 1958. Early satellites were propelled into space by rockets. Today, space shuttles also carry modern satellites into space.

In 1965, the first business satellite for communication, *Early Bird*, went into service. It could handle one television broadcast or 240 long-

Prehistory ——

500 B.C. ——

100 B.C. ——

A.D. 100 ——

200 ——

500 ——

1000 ——

1200 ——

1300 ——

1400 ——

1500 ——

1600 ——

1700 ——

1800 ——

1900 ——

2000 ——

2100 ——

Satellites use electromagnetic waves to receive radio, telephone, and television signals from one place and transmit them thousands of miles to another place.

distance phone calls at a time. *Early Bird* was a geostationary satellite.

Geostationary satellites orbit the earth 22,300 miles above the equator. They travel at the same speed as earth rotates on its axis. Because these satellites match earth's rotation, they are always above the same place on earth. The satellite always stays in range, which allows two or more ground stations to stay in constant contact. This makes them an ideal way to send radio, television, and telephone signals just about anywhere on earth. These satellites allow a person with a satellite phone to make a call or connect to the Internet from anywhere in the world.

A Prediction Come True

Science-fiction writer Arthur Clarke predicted the future of geostationary satellites in 1945. It took nearly twenty years for his ideas to become reality. NASA, the National Aeronautics and Space Administration, launched the first experimental geostationary communication satellite in 1963. President John F. Kennedy made history when he used it to make a satellite phone call from Washington to Nigeria.

23

Fax machines were invented soon after the telegraph, but it took about one hundred years before improvements helped them become popular.

Faxing History

Modern technology sometimes helps shape events as they are happening. For example, fax machines played a part in an uprising against the Chinese government in 1989 in Tiananmen Square in the city of Beijing. To the dismay of the Chinese government, demonstrators faxed news of their plans and of unfolding events to others within China and to other countries as well.

Faxes

"Fax" is short for *facsimile*, which means "to make similar." A fax machine takes a document and sends its image to another fax machine, which makes a replica of the original document.

A fax machine scans a document line by line from top to bottom. A fax machine will copy text, photographs, and other images. The fax machine breaks down each line of a document into many dots, called pixels. As it scans, the machine determines whether each line is black, because of text or some other image, or white, from the blank portions of the page. This information is converted into electrical signals. The electrical signals are transmitted by telephone to a receiving fax machine. The receiving fax machine converts the electrical signals back into a document and prints it.

A device called a modem converts the information into electrical signals for transmission. Because a fax machine uses a telephone line for transmission, the modem changes the electrical signals *into sound*. At the receiving end, the modem converts the signals back into data. People can send copies of letters, photographs, and drawings anywhere in the world with a telephone line and a fax machine.

Faxes are related to the telegraph. Crude versions were around for more than one hundred years before improvements came in the mid-1980s. They first became popular in businesses, then for personal use. Nowadays a fax machine may be built into a computer or may be a separate machine.

Fax machines use electrical signals to transmit an image by telephone from one fax machine to another.

Prehistory —

500 B.C. —

100 B.C. —

A.D. 100 —

200 —

500 —

1000 —

1200 —

1300 —

1400 —

1500 —

1600 —

1700 —

1800 —

1900 —

2000 —

2100 —

Pagers, Cordless Phones, and Cellular Phones

Cordless phones (above) use weak radio waves to link the phone to its base. A cell phone (below) acts as a radio transmitter and makes calls from almost anywhere.

In recent years, three inventions have made it possible to stay in touch from almost anywhere. These three inventions are pagers, cordless phones, and cellular phones.

A pager is a small device that lets a person know that someone wants to reach him or her. The pager beeps, buzzes, or vibrates when a caller dials the pager number on a telephone. A phone number to call or other short message appears on the pager screen. Pagers use a weak radio network to transmit information.

Cordless telephones also use radio technology. The antenna on the handset allows a cordless phone to be used away from its base. Weak radio waves link the phone to the base. As cordless phones have developed, the distance they can be used away from their base has increased, but they are still limited.

Cell phones are a combination of telephone, radio, and computer technology. Cell phones have been around since the early 1980s. They became increasingly popular beginning in the late 1990s.

A cell phone acts as a radio transmitter. When a cell phone user dials a number, the phone sends radio waves to a base station antenna. The antenna is located near the center of a geographical area called a cell. From the base station, signals travel to a switching office. From the switching office they are sent to either a local or long-distance telephone company. The telephone company transfers the signals to the number dialed, which may be either another cell phone or a regular phone. If the caller moves beyond the range of one cell, the signals transfer to the next nearby cell's base station. The system works in reverse if someone uses a regular phone to call a cell phone.

Cell phones are no longer used only for phone calls. They may also be used to send and receive e-mail, take pictures, and download music from the Internet, among other uses.

The popularity of cell phones exploded in the late 1990s and now they are also used for e-mail, to download music, and to take pictures.

E911

Lives have been saved when people have called 911 with cell phones. Sometimes, though, precious time is lost when a caller is unsure of his location. Enhanced 911 (E911) allows emergency workers to pinpoint a caller's location. E911 measures the time it takes for a cell call to reach three cell sites, computes where that call came from, and then provides the caller's location to emergency workers.

Prehistory

500 B.C.

100 B.C.

A.D. 100

200

500

1000

1200

1300

1400

1500

1600

1700

1800

1900

2000

2100

27

The U.S. government funded the Internet in the 1960s and now soldiers use e-mail to keep in touch with family back home.

The Internet and E-mail

The Internet is a huge computer network. It links millions of computers by telephone lines or other high-speed data lines. E-mail, which dates from the early 1970s, is a part of the Internet. People can use e-mail to send messages to other people who are thousands of miles away.

The Internet began in the 1960s as a project of the U.S. Department of Defense. The project, first called ARPANET and then later NSFNET, expanded at colleges and universities in the late 1980s. It provided a way for researchers to share their ideas.

Computer users connect to the Internet in a variety of ways. They may use their telephone line and a dial-up modem. A dial-up modem dials a phone number to connect to the Internet via telephone lines. A user may also connect with high-speed digital connections such as DSL, T1, T3, and cable modems. Most of these allow a computer to be connected to the Internet at all times, without tying up phone lines.

Information that travels over the Internet is divided into small numbered units called packets. These packets are sent out over many different routes. When the packets arrive at the receiving computer, they are put back together in order.

To send e-mail to another person, a user logs onto the Internet and opens an e-mail program. The user types in an e-mail address, the subject of the message, and the message itself. Pictures or other documents may be attached to the message before it is sent.

People need to use an e-mail program to retrieve their mail. An e-mail program usually uses a sound or picture, called an icon, to tell a user that mail has arrived. Until a user is logged in, messages are stored on servers or mail hosts.

FAST FACT

The Internet can also be used to carry telephone calls. This method is called Internet telephony.

With cell phones and computers, people can easily stay in touch and work from anywhere.

Prehistory —

500 B.C. —

100 B.C. —

A.D. 100 —

200 —

500 —

1000 —

1200 —

1300 —

1400 —

1500 —

1600 —

1700 —

1800 —

1900 —

2000 —

2100 —

World Wide Web and Instant Messaging

People use the Internet to find information, share pictures and videos, and send messages to each other.

The World Wide Web is part of the Internet. The Web, as it is often called, brings order to the Internet and makes it easy to get to information from it. The World Wide Web allows users to see color pictures and videos as well as text, and to hear sound on a Web page.

Before the creation of the Web, it was difficult for people to find information on the Internet. Tim Berners-Lee, creator of the Web, envisioned a web of documents where every user could see everyone else's work. The Web began in Switzerland as a way for nuclear physicists to share information. The World Wide Web was launched in August 1991.

Berners-Lee found a way to link information. When a computer user viewing a Web site clicks on an underlined or colored word or other linked item such as a photo, the computer displays information from another location. The linked location may be a different paragraph, a different page on the same site, or a different Web site completely. Berners-Lee also gave each Web page a special type of address.

To access the Web, a person needs an Internet connection and a browser. A browser is a computer program that displays information on the Web. Netscape Navigator and Microsoft's Internet Explorer are two popular browsers.

If users do not know where to find specific information, they go to Web sites called search engines. When a particular subject is typed

Prehistory —

500 B.C. —

100 B.C. —

A.D. 100 —

200 —

500 —

1000 —

1200 —

1300 —

1400 —

1500 —

1600 —

1700 —

1800 —

1900 —

2000 —

2100 —

into the engine, it lists Web sites related to that topic. Google is a popular search engine.

Instant messaging (IM) is another way to send messages from one computer to another. It differs from e-mail because IM works immediately. Instant messaging is like a telephone call, but it involves typing instead of talking. It allows two or more people who are online at the same time to instantly exchange typed messages.

From smoke signals to instant messaging, people have always looked for new ways to communicate over long distances. Today, the technology of long-distance communication changes almost daily, but the main goal has always remained the same: to connect people with one another throughout the world.

Instant messaging lets people all over the world connect with each other immediately.

Glossary

browser: A piece of software used to access the World Wide Web. It locates and displays Web pages.
courier: A messenger.
downlink: The transmission of signals from a satellite to earth.
electromagnetic waves: Electrical waves that travel through space.
geostationary satellite: A satellite that orbits the earth 22,300 miles above the equator and always appears above the same spot on earth.
graphics: Picture or other illustration. Graphics may be animated.
modem: Modulator-demodulator. A modem transfers informataion over telephone lines.
pictographs: A primitive writing where pictures represent ideas.
receiver: A device that changes incoming electromagnetic waves or electrical signals into audible or visual signals (signals that can be heard or seen).
scribe: A person who copied writing by hand before invention of the printing press.
transmitter: A device that sends radio or television signals using electromagnetic waves.
uplink: The transmission of electrical signals from earth to a satellite.

For More Information

Books

Sue Hamilton, *Communication: A Pictorial History of the Past One Thousand Years*. Edina, MN: Abdo & Daughters, 2000.
Alannah Hegedus, *Bleeps and Blips to Rocket Ships: Great Inventions in Communications*. Toronto, Canada: Tundra Books, 2001.
Thomas Streissguth, *Communications: Sending the Message*. Minneapolis, MN: Oliver, 1997.

Web Sites

Connected Earth (www.connected-earth.com). This site allows users to see all the parts inside communication devices, and how each part works.
A Science Odyssey (www.pbs.org/wgbh/aso). This site includes activities and information about inventions, technology, and the people behind them.

Index